LEVEL **1**

YOU READ · I READ

Animal Doctors

Libby Romero

NATIONAL GEOGRAPHIC

Washington, D.C.

How to Use This Book

Reading together is fun! When older and younger readers share the experience, it opens the door to new learning. As you read together, talk about what you learn.

YOU READ

This side is for a parent, older sibling, or older friend. Before reading each page, take a look at the words and pictures. Talk about what you see. Point out words that might be hard for the younger reader.

Many vets **examine**, or look at, family pets. These vets give pets checkups in animal clinics and hospitals. Other vets help animals on farms, in or near the ocean, at zoos, or at rescue centers.

Sometimes people bring animals to vets. Vets **examine** lots of animals in the wild, too!

I READ

This side is for the younger reader.

As you read, look for the bold words. Talk about them before you read.

At the end of each chapter, do the activity together.

YOUR TURN!

Name each animal. Then name the body part the pet vet is examining.

1

2

3

4

Contents

CHAPTER 1

Vets to the Rescue

YOU READ

A veterinarian is a doctor who takes care of animals. These doctors are also called **vets**. Vets take care of animals that are sick or hurt. They take care of healthy animals, too.

You go to your doctor for checkups. Animals get checkups, too! They go to the **vet**.

Doctors **help** people in many ways. They give medicines. They fix broken bones. They give shots. Sometimes they operate when people are sick or hurt. Vets do the same things for animals.

Vets also give people tips about how to take care of their animals. They **help** people learn how to keep animals healthy.

7

Many vets **examine**, or look at, family pets. These vets give pets checkups in animal clinics and hospitals. Other vets help animals on farms, in or near the ocean, at zoos, or at rescue centers.

Sometimes people bring animals to vets. Vets **examine** lots of animals in the wild, too!

YOUR TURN!

Where would a vet examine each of these animals? Match each animal to the place it might see a vet.

1 guinea pig

2 whale

3 chicken

4 tiger

A

farm

animal clinic

B

zoo

C

D

ocean

CHAPTER 2

Pet Vets

Max is a puppy. He goes to the pet vet for a checkup. Puppies need lots of checkups. The vet helps make sure Max grows up **healthy**.

Pet vets keep pets **healthy**. They give the pets shots to keep them from getting sick. They do tests. They may even test a pet's poop!

Pet vets check an animal from the top of its head to the tip of its tail. They listen to the pet's heart and lungs. They watch it move to make sure its **bones** and brain are healthy.

 Pet vets show people how to brush their pet's teeth. They also tell them what to feed their pet so its **bones** will be strong.

Sometimes pets swallow things they shouldn't. Uh-oh! It's time to go to the emergency clinic. The pet vet at the clinic uses different **machines** to see inside the pet's body.

The x-ray **machines** show what's inside the pet! Now the vet can help the pet.

toy

17

Pet vets handle all sorts of **problems**. If a cat breaks its leg or a hamster hurts its eye, a pet vet will know how to help.

Cats love to scratch chairs. A vet can tell you how to solve **problems** like this, too.

YOUR TURN!

Name each animal. Then name the body part the pet vet is examining.

1

2

ANSWERS: 1: dog, ear; 2: cat, teeth; 3: parrot, heart; 4: rabbit, eye

CHAPTER 3

Farm Vets

YOU READ

Nancy is a horse.
She lives on a farm.
Her **hooves** grow just like
your fingernails do. When they
get too long, her feet hurt. The farm
vet comes to trim her hooves.

22

Farm vets take care of animals on farms. They check each animal from its horns to its **hooves**.

23

Farm vets may drive a long way to get from one farm to the next. Sometimes they come to help one animal, like Nancy. Other times they take care of a **group** of animals on a farm.

Farm vets check each animal in the **group**. If one animal is sick, the whole group can get sick.

Taking care of a lot of animals is hard work for a farmer. Farm vets help farmers make a **plan**. The plan helps farmers keep track of their animals' health and growth.

The **plan** tells farmers what the animals should eat. It says how much they should eat, too.

27

YOU READ Many farm animals are born in the spring. A farm vet can come to help the mother animals have their babies. This pig has eight **piglets**.

The vet checks the **piglets**.
She checks the mother
pig, too.

YOUR TURN!

Make a plan to keep your favorite farm animal healthy.

- Draw a picture of your favorite farm animal.
- Make a list of foods the animal should eat.
- Say how the animal will get exercise.
- Draw a picture of the animal's home.

CHAPTER 4

Wild Animal Vets

YOU
READ

Jojo is a baby gorilla. Gorillas live in the **wild**. Jojo's mother lived in the wild until she got hurt. She was taken to a zoo to get better. Jojo was born in the zoo. Someday, he and his mother may go back to the wild.

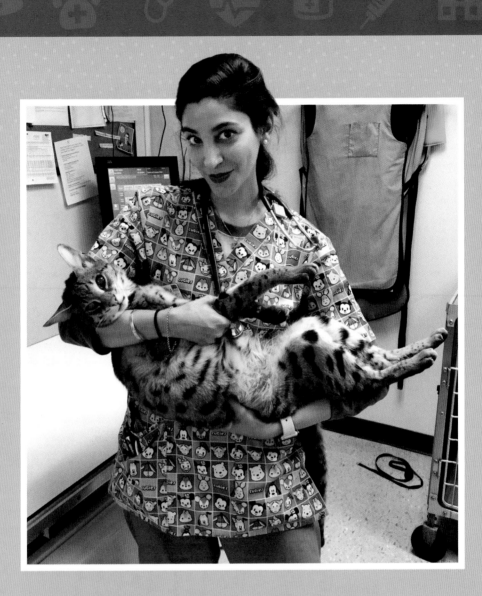

Wild animal vets study animals where they live. Some also help take care of wild animals in zoos.

YOU READ The wild animal vets use their experience with animals at the zoo to help animals in the wild. If they find a hurt wild gorilla, they may give it the same **treatment**, or medicine, that helped Jojo's mother.

At the zoo, vets learn the best **treatments** to keep animals healthy.

YOU READ

Not all wild animals live in places that are far away. Some live near you! **Birds** are wild animals. Just like you might break your arm, a bird can break its wing or beak. A wild animal vet can fix it.

When the **bird** is better, the wild animal vet lets it go back into the wild.

YOUR TURN!

squirrel

bird

frog

Take a walk in your neighborhood with a grown-up. What wild animals do you see? Take notes in a journal or notebook.

CHAPTER 5

Ocean Animal Vets

 YOU READ

Fay is a sea turtle. She lives in the **ocean**. A boat hit Fay, and she got a cut on her neck. People took Fay to a clinic at an ocean animal rescue center.

Ocean animal vets help animals in the water, on the beach, and in clinics.

YOU READ

Ocean animal vets return most animals like Fay to the wild. But sometimes animals are too sick or injured to return to the wild. The vets keep these animals in an **aquarium** and take care of them there.

I READ

When the sick or hurt animals feel better, they may get lots of visitors at the **aquarium**.

YOU READ Ocean animal vets also work with people. They show people how to take care of the ocean. They tell them to recycle and not litter. This keeps the water clean and **protects** the ocean animals.

If we **protect** the ocean, we protect the animals that live in it. We help vets keep the animals healthy.

YOUR TURN!

Pick your favorite ocean animal. Tell a story about the animal. How could you teach people to protect the animal?

sea star

orca

shark

clownfish

octopus

For Clocktower Animal Hospital, Herndon, VA —L.R.

Published by National Geographic Partners, LLC, Washington, DC 20036.

Designed by Gus Tello

The author and publisher gratefully acknowledge the expert content review of this book by Dr. Gabby Wild and the literacy review of this book by Kimberly Gillow, principal, Chelsea School District, Michigan.

Photo Credits

Abbreviations: AS = Adobe Stock; GI = Getty Images
Cover (CTR), Jose Luis Pelaez Inc/GI; 1, Kurhan/AS; 3, BraunS/GI; 4-5, FatCamera/GI; 4 (LE), Penny Tweedie/GI; 4-45 (header art) (UP), davooda/AS; 4-45 (header art) (UP), Valentyna/AS; 5 (UP RT), antoine-photographe/AS; 6, santypan/AS; 7, pressmaster/AS; 8, 135pixels/AS; 9, AP Photo/Aditya Sutanta/Abaca Press/Sipa USA; 10-11 (LO), thammanoon/AS; 10 (UP LE), devmarya/AS; 10 (UP RT), Craig Lambert Photo/AS; 10 (LO LE), TTstudio/AS; 11 (UP LE), Bob/AS; 11 (UP RT), Tyler Olson/AS; 11 (CTR), Iriana Shiyan/AS; 11 (LO RT), peangdao/AS; 12-13, Monkey Business/AS; 12 (LO), Karoline Thalhofer/AS; 14, Rido/AS; 15, Pixel-Shot/AS; 16, herraez/GI; 17 (LO), Hybrid Images/GI; 17 (UP), Monty Rakusen/GI; 18 (LO LE), irishasel/AS; 18 (UP RT), daniel rajszczak/AS; 19, Juniors Bildarchiv/F314/Alamy Stock Photo; 20-21 (CTR), Africa Studio/AS; 20 (LE), Alexander Raths/AS; 21 (UP LE), New Africa/AS; 21 (LO RT), kaew6566/AS; 22 (UP), Angelov/AS; 22 (LO RT), hedgehog94/Shutterstock; 23, 1001color/AS; 24-25, Reimar/AS; 25 (LO RT), eric/AS; 26, only_kim/Shutterstock; 27, Habman18/AS; 28, Martine De Graaf/Dreamstime; 29, FotoSabine/AS; 30-31 (CTR), czarny_bez/AS; 30-31 (LO), larisa_zorina/AS; 30-31, Charles Brutlag/Dreamstime; 31 (UP RT), czarny_bez/AS; 32, gudkovandrey/AS; 33, Gabby Wild; 34, Cyril Ruoso/Minden Pictures; 35 (UP RT), Zoological Society of San Diego/Handout/GI; 35 (CTR LE), Brent Stirton/National Geographic Image Collection; 35 (LO RT), Sirachai Arunrugstichai/Nature Picture Library; 36, Nikki Herbst/Shutterstock; 37, Leonard Ortiz/MediaNews Group/Orange County Register/Contributor/GI; 38-39, kate_sept2004/GI; 38 (LO LE), Martin/AS; 39 (UP), nd700/AS; 39 (LO), Opayaza/AS; 40, vladislav333222/AS; 41, Chris Johnson/Alamy Stock Photo; 42-43, Justin Guariglia/National Geographic Image Collection; 43 (LO RT), kali9/GI; 44, Danita Delimont/Alamy Stock Photo; 45, Richard Whitcombe/Shutterstock; 46 (UP LE), Damsea/Shutterstock; 46, Tory Kallman/Shutterstock; 47 (UP LE), VisionDive/Shutterstock; 47 (CTR RT), Tommy Schultz/AS; 47 (LO RT), OceanBodhi/iStockphoto/GI

Library of Congress Cataloging-in-Publication Data

Names: Romero, Libby, author.
Title: Animal doctors / Libby Romero.
Description: Washington : National Geographic Kids, 2023. | Series: National geographic readers | Audience: Ages 4-6 | Audience: Grades K-1
Identifiers: LCCN 2021047244 | ISBN 9781426373640 (paperback) | ISBN 9781426374388 (library binding)
Subjects: LCSH: Veterinarians--Juvenile literature.
Classification: LCC SF756 .R66 2023 | DDC 636.089/069--dc23/eng/20211014
LC record available at https://lccn.loc.gov/2021047244

Printed in the United States of America
22/WOR/1